HOW TO SUCCESSFULLY SELF-PUBLISH YOUR BOOKS

A complete guide to earn money from your books and fetch a steady passive income from your writing as an aspiring or already self-published author, without traditional or vanity publishers.

IREDAFENEVESHO OWOLABI

Copyright © Iredafenevesho Owolabi 2020

Some other Fast-selling Books By the author are:

- Kingdom Verities
- How to Enjoy Kingdom Currency (Vol. 1)
- How to Maximize Kingdom Currency (Vol. 2)
- Kingdom Currency for Students, Graduates and Businessmen (Vol. 3)
- Unlocking Your Kingdom Creativity
- 4-D THINKING
- Why you should Write a Book
- How to Turn your Knowledge to Money
- How to Turn Wisdom Currency to Money'
- How to Make Millions as an Author-preneur
- 18 Steps to Writing a Book Successfully
- How to Launch, Sell and Market your Books Profitably

TABLE OF CONTENT

INTRODUCTION

Not every author who completes a manuscript goes on to publish the content they've put countless hours of research, thought and effort into. It is reported that of 1000 people who start writing, only 30 of them finish the book and out of that figure, just 6 of them end up publishing it. This is because most people do not know what to do with their written work due to several factors. For some, their hindrance could be financial constraints, lack of knowledge, misinformation and fear of the unknown. This book would help you with proper guide on how best to publish your book whether your concern is availability of money, improper understanding of the process involved, the seeming complexity of the machinery involved or fear. The next few points would help you on your journey as a

self-published author-preneur.

CHAPTER ONE

DO I NEED AN ISBN?

A lot of writers do not know the importance of having an ISBN for their book. Having an International Standard Book Number (ISBN) adds some professional touch to your book and makes it identifiable anywhere in the world based on the number it is assigned. An ISBN is used by publishers, booksellers and libraries for ordering, listing and stock control activities. It allows a specific publisher to be identified. It also makes it possible for a specific publisher to identify a particular edition of a certain title and the specific format used for the book. If you do not want your book to be sold by commercial vendors like local and international bookstores, wholesalers, retailers, e-commerce platforms, then you could do without an ISBN. However, I would strongly advise against that because you stand a huge risk with that approach. This is because most retailers and book distributors will insist that your book has an ISBN before they would consider selling or marketing it. Books that are sold through bookshops and online retailers almost always require an International Standard Book Number (ISBN). This is their way of ensuring order processing is completed smoothly, reliably and cost effectively. Therefore, you greatly limit yourself and would only be able to sell your books yourself without an ISBN. An ISBN does not provide any form of legal or copyright protection to your work. To protect your work, you would need to catalogue it with the Library of Congress.

Apart from providing access to marketing tools that can help with sales of your book, an ISBN also provides direct access to library databases. These databases are organized by ISBN and are used by libraries and book trade organizations to provide timely information to customers. For me, whether I am having a paperback print edition or an eBook, I get an ISBN because of the opportunities it affords to my books. You can get one from a publisher but the name of the company who gives it to you would need to be on the book as the publisher. This also obtains even when they did not contribute any other thing to the publishing of your book. If you want your own name or personal publishing outfit to be recognized for the publishing, then you would need to get an ISBN block. In some countries, it is cheaper to buy an ISBN block than to buy just one ISBN from another publisher. Find what works for you, and do

it!

CHAPTER TWO

WHAT BOOK FORMATS SHOULD I USE?

If you want to reach out to people in the different strata of society who possess a variety of preferences, then your book should at least be available in different formats. This would help partly because different e-commerce book selling sites have specific formats in which every book it distributes should be presented. In addition to that, I have discovered from my experience, sometimes the preferences of readers vary from one age range to another. For example, those who are more elderly and within the ages of 45-70 and above prefer to read printed formats of a book. They could also embrace the idea of an audio cd of your book especially if they have cars in which they could listen to these CDs. On the other hand, people of the younger generation are more open to the idea of buying or reading eBooks because they have digital devices and are on these devices almost all day. This is not exclusively true for all but for most of these individuals. Nowadays, to reach out to the younger generation, you need to be adapted to ways you can get their attention while they are on their digital devices.

How to Format your Manuscript into an E-Book

If you intend to sell your book only as an eBook, you can convert the completed word file into PDF format. If you would love to do this, follow these guidelines. These steps apply to you if you have completed your manuscript and have proof-read it. For Microsoft Office users, just go to "file" on the far-left top corner of your screen and then click "Save As" (in case you do not find it there, look around the screen and click "Save As"). After that, enter the title of your book and click "save as type" below the "file name" you just edited. Then go ahead and select the format you want to save the file in which is PDF. Once you click the button to select PDF as file save format, your manuscript would be converted to PDF.

If you want something more arranged with a particular size in mind and you really do not know how to format it from Microsoft document to a PDF file, no worries, you can get it done for you by a freelancer. Just go to www.fiverr.com, find someone credible and tell them what you want. You should also get a mobi file and an epub file if you want your eBook to be sold on e-commerce platforms apart from your website/download link. Just go to fiverr and tell a competent freelancer you are convinced to work with what you want. You would get something good as long as you select a competent seller on the platform. Before choosing a freelancer, look at the reviews on his profile. Avoid using new sellers on fiverr. Look out for either a level two seller or a level one seller with a credible work history.

PS: You should be careful not to fall into the hands of amateurs there.

CHAPTER THREE

EXPLORE YOUR PUBLISHING OPTIONS STRATEGICALLY

Before going to a printing press or a publisher you must weigh your options properly. Before deciding to print "xyz" number of books or to use any automated system, you need to consider your options in a strategic manner. For instance, if you are not sure whether 200-500 people would buy your book after printing, then the clever thing to do is to produce it as an eBook for starters. With the kind of responses and feedbacks you get from those who buy and read the digital copy, you can know whether to go ahead with producing the printed version or to hold on. Timing is very critical and must be seriously considered in making these decisions. When is it right to run a print of 1,000 copies, when is it right to run a print of 5,000 copies or more? Should I even print this book at all? Can I afford to print these books now? Do I have the customer base to buy at least half of these books yet? Should I use print-on-demand instead? All these are very important questions you must answer as an author-preneur before committing hard-earned money to printing.

An author without business sense does not care, all he wants is to attain the status of having his or her books in print (which is not a bad idea). However, if you do not want your money to be lost to publishers, you must think differently as an author-preneur would. An author-preneur studies the market and knows when it is time to print and when not to print. He knows whether to go with selling the digital copy first before considering the hard copy production.

Benefits of Making an E-Book

The good thing about an eBook is that you are not under any pressure to sell them because you have nothing to lose in the event that people refuse to buy. Even though there are people who would not buy an eBook but prefer to get the hard copy, it is advisable to be sure your numbers are right before committing huge funds to printing. I know of people who spent millions to print over 10,000 books and after production, could not sell more than 100 copies. Those books are collecting dust somewhere in an apartment now. I also know people who borrowed hundreds of thousands to print books which they are unable to sell because nobody knows them.

Before printing books, you must have built a good customer base, reputation or following. If you do not have any of these, then it is advisable you start with the digital copy while you build a loyal tribe who end up becoming an army of buyers.

Producing an eBook is wonderful because you do not have to bother about printing cost. Another benefit in an eBook is that if you discover errors after publishing, it can easily be corrected without any major issue or loss. All you need do is trace the error back to the word document from which the PDF was generated and effect the corrections. However, if you've spent hundreds of thousands printing a book that has a major error like a spelling error in your name, title or content; or a technical error in the arrangement, layout or page numbering, your printed book would not be excellent. It may therefore become difficult to correct such mistakes (such mistakes can be avoided with thorough scrutiny and proof-reading though). You would be faced with these 4 options: to destroy the books, sell them like that, get a refund or do a reprint at your expense, the publisher's expense or both. All these headaches can be avoided by producing an eBook and if any error is noticed, all you need do is go back to the Microsoft document and effect the correction. Ultimately, whether it is an eBook or print book, make sure you proof-read thoroughly to avoid errors before publishing.

Instead of enriching a publisher or printing press with hundreds of thousands in printing books for which you do not have buyers, it is advisable to produce digital copies. One thing about eBooks that I find interesting is if 1,000 people buy a digital book, it does not deplete in quantity. It means that just one eBook that you produced could be sold thousands and even millions of times. You do not need to go back and print more copies when you have sold a particular number of copies except you feel like running a printed version of your eBook.

On the other hand, if you have decided to print your books, that is a welcome idea so long as you have done your homework. One thing I must advise you about is before striking a deal with a publisher or printing press you should do your research and make your own findings to be sure you are printing or publishing your books at a very fair bargain. For instance, if you want to print a number of copies for your title, make sure you ask more than one printer for a quotation. Even after getting estimates from different printers, do your own underground work by trying to find out how much items like reams of papers cost. Also make sure you are dealing with someone who is capable of doing for you a good quality print. If you fail to research the prices of different printers, you may lose valuable time and money when issues arise. You may get a poorly performed job full of mistakes or get cheated. I have singlehandedly supervised the printing and publishing of over 8,000 books from several different publishers and have seen many errors in production which I have been able to successfully avoid since my first printing experience. Most of these errors come from using an incompetent hand, a faulty machine or low-quality materials. That is why it is important to look carefully before you leap into the laps of any printer or publisher.

1.   **E-Book publishing**:

This is a very wonderful way you can publish your book. There is a massive ever-growing market for digital products in our world today. You have to be living in the caves to not know that you need to make your books available on digital format. The way I see it is that in a skyscraper for example, printed books are like the staircase while eBooks are like the elevators. If you truly want to enjoy the money-making potentials of writing and publishing a book, then your best bet is to publish it in a digital format. E-Books cannot replace the print version of a book but they are easier and quicker to spread and distribute. That is not to say print books are less important. They are both alternatives that cannot totally displace the relevance of each other. However, it is easier for your eBook to go viral than for a print version to do so because of the leverage the internet and social media has made available. Another advantage is that you do not require so much money to produce an eBook as you may require for a print book except you have a sponsor or a publishing contract.

One of the fears and biases some authors have for eBooks is that people could send their eBooks to others who did not pay for the book. I used to think in that same manner until I came to a better understanding of how things work. Even if people transfer your book to others without payment, they are helping you spread your name and your message. It should not bother you because they cannot send it to everybody in the world. There are 8 billion people on the planet and all you need is a minute percentage or fraction to make your millions. Anyone who gets your eBook for free from someone who bought yours would be blessed to receive of your value and may even subscribe to your services afterwards. Remember that your major goal as an author-preneur is not to sell your books but to build a brand that gets you paid, seen, read and heard. You could also program your eBook in a way that it can only be accessed through the device with which it was downloaded after it was paid for. However, I think there is no need for that if you really want your message to go out there. You would be caging your message by yourself if you did that.

CHAPTER FOUR

HOW TO SELL YOUR EBOOK WITHOUT A WEBSITE

One great way to sell your eBook is to have a website, do not be deceived. If you really want to build a business and a solid brand around your writing craft, you need one. Nevertheless, you can also sell it without a website. To sell your eBook without a website, you need a downloadable link. To get a downloadable link, upload your PDF file to www.googledrive.com. Afterwards, copy the link of the file you uploaded on google drive and go to a website known as "bit.ly" to shorten and customize your google drive link. When that is done you can sell your eBook to people. To make this very effective, use www.paystack.com to create a payment page. With that page once people pay via the Paystack link, they are immediately redirected to where they can download your book (especially for Nigerian authors).

What if People do not buy because it is not a printed book?

It is true that most people prefer to buy hard copy books than eBooks but it is only a matter of value system. If their value perception of your eBook is straightened up, you would get these same people to buy the digital books they once rejected. Therefore, it is your job to enlighten them and give them reasons to try your eBooks despite that they were used to hard copies previously. The most common reason why people prefer the hard copy of a book title is, they can write on the book while reading. People like to mark a book here and there while studying it. But most times, after they finish reading the book, they forget what they marked on it and what they wrote down on the book. I used to be like that until I started taking notes on a separate notepad when reading and found it to be a more effective means of taking notes. Therefore, when I read books now, whether hard or soft copy, I take notes on a separate notepad in a way I can always refer to it in the future. Before I jot down, I just make a heading with the title of the book I am reading. This has been more beneficial as I get to always revise my notes from time to time.

When I wrote my 5th book, it took me over 1,000 hours to write, proof-read and edit it. That also included fine tuning and perfecting it for final production. I poured in hours of research as I churned out about 71, 220 words into this 215-page book. Most of my customers and clients loved the idea of producing it solely as an eBook. They said they preferred it because it was easier to buy and access it on the go through their digital devices. A few others who were already accustomed to my print books however, were in shock because they only value a book when it is in print. *How did I deal with this?* All I did was to show them that an eBook was also a real book; just that it happened to be in digital format. After showing them that an eBook was as valuable as the physical book, their value system changed. They therefore went ahead to purchase my new eBook and my other eBooks. Now they appreciate the fact that an eBook is easier to access and contains as much value as the physical one. Mind you, the eBook cannot replace the physical print because they both have their advantages and disadvantages just like the elevator cannot replace the staircase in a skyscraper. They are both alternatives and it is your duty as an author-preneur to educate your potential clients who are traditionally bound to reading only print books. By enlightening them, they could learn to accept your digital books if your print books are not available and would be better for it.

CHAPTER FIVE

AMAZON INDIE PUBLISHING

Indie publishing is another term for self-publishing. There are several ways to go about indie publishing and Amazon is the most popular of them all.

a. Kindle Publishing:

Amazon kindle controls about 70% of the e-commerce book market as at the time of this writing. So, if you really want some leverage, then you need to also consider having your books on Amazon kindle store. Just go to www.kdp.amazon.com and get started. It is that easy once you can create an Amazon account and it costs nothing to do these except you are paying a third party to do it for you. If you do not want a third party, then you can do it yourself. Just go to www.kdp.amazon.com and sign in. You would need a foreign account through which you would receive payments when your book is purchased on Amazon. The good thing is you can get a foreign account for this purpose without opening a domiciliary account in a physical bank. There are several online payment service providers whose platforms are compatible with Amazon payment portal. You can go to www.payooneer.com to open a foreign account at no initial cost. You would get a Payooneer MasterCard sent to you at an address you provide. If you reside in Nigeria for example, it would be couriered to you and you can get it within a very short period of at least two weeks depending on the current policy they operate by. Immediately you open the account, you would get different foreign account numbers. Once you have the account number, you can link it up to your Amazon account which you set up. Then you can upload your books for sales on Amazon Kindle. To upload your books on KDP, you should convert the final manuscript from word document to a mobi file or other Amazon KDP-friendly formats.

b. Print on Demand-Publishing:

Amazon has a Print-on-Demand service which was formerly called CreateSpace publishing (www.createspace.com). Before this writing, CreateSpace and Kindle Direct Publishing operated as different entities under Amazon, but the last time I checked, that has changed. At this writing, CreateSpace has being moved to KDP such that they are now both under the same roof so to speak. Since this move has been completed, you can now access the Amazon Print-on-Demand service on the same site and platform with its KDP services via www.kdp.amazon.com.

Print-on-Demand means that your books only get printed when a customer places order for them and pays for them. It takes great pressure off your shoulder as an author. You do not necessarily have to print your books with vague expectations that someone somewhere would buy them. This approach ties your printing capital down for too long. With this strategic approach to self-publishing, Amazon prints and delivers your book on your behalf. It takes its time to distribute the printed copy of your book to a buyer who orders for it in countries like USA, United Kingdom, Canada, Australia, Brazil, Denmark, etc. I am a first-hand witness of the benefit of this facility and it has really fetched me a handsome reward since

I began using it some years ago. To get your books on this platform, your file must be converted to a PDF file. Amazon allows different file sizes but the standard file size that gets the largest range of distribution is the 6×9 inch size. Your cover design should also be in PDF with a little allowance on the edges for trimming.

c. Amazon ACX:

On this platform, you get to sell your audio books. The audio book however must be in sync with the written book and that may require a professional voice over to be achieved. There are professional narrators and producers on this platform that can do the voicing for you. You can use them if you are okay with their pricing or find other options that soothe your budget.

IngramSpark:

This platform is the largest book distribution network for indie authors and publishers at this writing. They achieved this through a handful of strategic global partnerships with several outlets like online stores, E-book retailers, libraries, schools, universities, local niche retailers, big chains, little chains and indie bookstores. It is a company that has the trust of over 39,000 retailers, libraries, distributors, and educational institutions worldwide. They supply books to these different vendors on a Print-on-Demand basis. So, if you have your books on this platform, you stand a great chance of having your books across these multiple retail platforms across the globe. They offer speedy direct shipping and reliable global delivery to different countries around the world. These retailers order your books at a wholesale price set by you or your publisher and they pay for them while IngramSpark prints and supplies them to them. They remove their service charge and printing cost leaving you with the rest as your profit. On this platform, you are the one who decides how much you want your books to be sold for. The beauty of all these platforms for me is not just the great potential it provides you to make lots of money. Rather it is the great and massive structure they have to help you get your books as far and wide as possible. IngramSpark also distributes your eBooks to over 100 platforms that sell digital books like iTunes, kobobooks, etc. The advantage of this is that instead of putting your book in these different digital book platforms one after the other,

IngramSpark distributes your books to them on your behalf.

CHAPTER SIX

VANITY PUBLISHING/SELF-PUBLISHING

It is no longer news that aspiring authors find it difficult to get published by traditional publishers. This is because a traditional publisher looks at your manuscript and has to be fully persuaded that it is worth investing in before he picks it up. Once they see the financial prospect of your manuscript, they bear the responsibility of publishing, selling and marketing your books without a dime from you. That is the reason they most times only do this for popular authors or some newbie who has succeeded in attracting their attention because it is more likely to sell big and quick. They do not put their resources on a book that might not sell in their opinion (most times they assume wrongly). Vanity publishers on the other hand print your books at your direct expenses. You bear the cost of printing, publishing, marketing and selling your printed books all by yourself. Vanity publishing is commonly used by authors who are not popular or who do not have a traditional publisher that would give them a publishing agreement. The focus of this book is actually to help people in this category. Many of such independent self-published authors are victims of so many unfair events that dim their hopes for profiting due to vanity publishers. These publishers are only interested in making profit off your neck and never help you market or distribute your books hence they leave authors with a huge pile of books they cannot sell.

Genuine self-publishers on the other hand are not as greedy as vanity publishers. They make it clear how much each service costs and what the money is being spent on. Some even assist the author with distribution among other services. They also give the author control of the process unlike the vanity publishers. The sad truth is that most of these vanity publishers call themselves self-publishers and make the journey more difficult for self-published authors.

In Nigeria, what we have is mostly Vanity publishers posing as Self-publishers. One of the challenges people in this part of the world face is with getting a good printing press that can give a good quality print at a fair bargain. Most times, when these printers discover or notice that you do not know much about printing, they tend to charge exorbitant prices and give bloated estimates. The innocent, naïve and desperate aspiring author is then left with little or no options but to either bury his manuscript for lack of funds or pay outrageous fees just to get their books printed.

I remember my first printed book project and how I was a victim of this. Immediately my book had been proof-read and was fit for production, I made contact with several printers. I finally settled for the "cheapest" of them all. This printer gave me a very bogus quotation and because I was new in the system, I did not have a clue that he was cheating me. He made me feel like he was doing me a huge favour, little did I know that he was exploiting my shallow knowledge of the book production process. When I questioned the price estimates he gave me, he simply told me some jargons that further confused me. He justified his quotation with lies and told me that my book job required him to use 50 reams of paper and that was why I was charged that way. I really was new to all the terminologies and how the production was being calculated so I ignorantly agreed to his offer and blindly paid him on those exorbitant terms. To start with, he did not give me a good quality print because I ended up rejecting the books. Also, it was several months later I discovered that it was actually 20 reams of paper I ought to have paid for because that was what was needed. It then dawned on me that I was scammed of about ₦200,000 in that project because I lacked the understanding of the processes. This is minus the actual amount which I also paid for the job and service charges. Yes, that is ridiculous!

You see, when you do not know anything about printing in this part of the world, most printers would exploit you mercilessly and that was my case. In a more decent setting or in the western world, this may not be the case. But thank heavens that at the end of it all I was able to sell all my books profitably in a short space of time (thanks to strategic book marketing). If not, it would have been really bad! Can you imagine that it was when I was to do a reprint of the same book, I discovered that I had been hoodwinked by the previous printer? Some people may never even discover in a lifetime. That is why I advise that you know at least the basics of printing if you intend to use vanity printers to produce your books. There are many things you must know if you want to break even as an author-preneur especially in this part of the world. If it takes asking someone knowledgeable to coach you on these processes, please do whatever it takes. If not, you would labour, do hundreds of hours of research, spend months to write your book and yet, your printer is the one who gets to be enriched after all. This can be avoided with proper mentoring or thorough research.

After that experience, I invested time and money in coaching sessions that walked me through the book production process. I got someone who taught me how the whole book production process takes place and how to know a fair bargain when I see one. That was when I learned how to ascertain how many reams of paper would be required to print a given number of books, how many lithographic plates would be required per a given number of books, among other technical details of the printing process. It was an eye-opener for me and since my first encounter no printer has succeeded in charging me outrageously again. Below are some basics that you should know about while printing your books in this

part of the world.

CHAPTER SEVEN

STEPS FOR PRINTING YOUR BOOKS IN THE VANITY PUBLISHING PRESS

Based on my knowledge of the steps involved in printing a book, whenever I want to print books, I already know how much is required for the job. So, I get to give the printers what they deserve for the job, no more no less. There are different methods for printing a book. One method could be the use of digital printing machine. This method produces better quality and is used mostly when you are printing very few copies. Amazon uses this method to fulfil their print-on-demand orders since it does not print them in bulk. There are other non-digital machines which are more suited for bulk printing.

Below, I would give a simplistic summary of how the printing is done. This applies whether a digital printing machine or a non-digital one is being used. This should give you an overall idea of how most books are produced. This knowledge is important because among other things, it would make it difficult for a printer to deceive you. Below are the basic steps involved:

i. Formatting:

At this stage, your book is formatted and arranged into a layout in such a way that when the layout is printed on a sheet and folded, it would be properly formed and fitted into a book. It is in this stage you would be able to ascertain how many pages your manuscript would be when it is printed as a book. Once you know the number of pages, you should be able to calculate how many reams of paper, plates, and other estimates needed to complete your project. The wise thing to do is to know how many pages your book would be after printing before agreeing on a price. This kind of formatting is usually done with Corel Draw software or any other related computer application.

ii. Production of Lithographic Plates:

This is the next step after formatting and curving the interior of the book. Here, it is transferred into a plate called a lithographic plate. This is a metal plate that is used to transfer ink to paper. And this is what would be used to print what you have written into a bond paper. This can be done directly from computer to plate with a digital machine. Alternatively, it could be done manually from computer to film to plate.

The former is more effective, more accurate and usually faster. The number of lithographic plates that would be required for your book is dependent on the number of pages your book was formatted into.

iii. Impression:

At the impression stage, the plates are inserted into the machine, and reams of the bond paper are arranged into the machine. At this point, the words you wrote in your manuscript are impressed on the sheets of paper. At the impression stage, the interior of your book would be printed in large sheets of an A1 or A2 sized paper depending on the machine being used. The prices of the bond papers to be used for impression varies depending on the thickness and the economics prevalent in the market per time. The recommended thickness for your book should be anything from 70 grams and above. Some printers use 60 grams but the books would not come out as it would if you use 70-100 grams. Also, the number of reams that would be required is dependent on the number of lithographic plates that came out in the previous step. The number of books to be printed also affects how many reams of paper should do the job. It would help if you can know some of these details. They may look technical, but if you really want to profit from book printing, you should have an idea and a basic understanding of these. Otherwise, you may be cheated by printers in an outrageous manner.

iv. Cover Page Printing:

After the impression stage, the cover page is printed on a thicker kind of paper different from the one used for the interiors (250 grams and above is recommended). This can be done with a digital printer or other machines that can print in four colours.

v. Cover Page Lamination:

After printing the cover page, it is laminated. There are two kinds of lamination. Glossy laminate and Matte laminate. Choose whichever one suits you and let your printer know your preferences. They both have their different feel and different prices also. Select your preferences and let your printer know the type of lamination you want for the job.

vi. Finishing:

At this stage, the printed sheets at the impression phase are collated and folded in a way that is serially arranged by page numbering. If this stage is not done properly, the pages may not be serially arranged or some pages may come out up-side-down.

vii. Hot Binding:

This is the stage of joining the interior of the book and the laminated book cover and passing it through the binding machine. By doing this, the book gets thoroughly glued at the spine.

viii. Cutting:

After binding the books, they go through the cutting machine for trimming and removing rough edges. This gives the book a smooth outlook.

These are the basic steps that your book would likely go through before it becomes a finished product. In each step, there are some fundamental best practices a printer must observe for the book to come out excellently. A mistake or oversight in one step can go a long way to negatively impact the overall finished product. That is why it is advisable to not take chances when making a choice on whom to print your books as a self-published or vanity published author.

ABOUT THE AUTHOR

My name is Iredafenevesho Owolabi (Iredafe or Dafe for short). I am a Creativity Coach with the goal of helping individuals and organizations move from idea to profitable creations. I redefine public speaking with cutting-edge kingdom insights. I am happily married to the love of my life and together we are affecting lives.

My books are being read in different parts of the world with countless testimonials of their impact. From my experience and results as a self-published author-preneur of more than 10 books in hard copies, soft copies, audio version, and many different formats, I have learned the tricks of the self-publishing trade.

I mentor several aspiring authors to success via my coaching calls and my book titled "How to Make Millions as An Author-preneur" is a must-have for all authors and aspiring author-preneurs who intend to master the business of their writing gift. This book is a gift from me to the self-publishing industry and would help you as a starter, intermediate or advanced writer.